United States Presidents

Jimmy Carter

Paul Joseph
ABDO Publishing Company

visit us at
www.abdopub.com

Published by Abdo Publishing Company 4940 Viking Drive, Edina, Minnesota 55435.
Copyright © 1999 by Abdo Consulting Group, Inc. International copyrights reserved in
all countries. No part of this book may be reproduced in any form without written
permission from the publisher.

Printed in the United States.

Cover and Interior Photo credits: AP/Wide World, Archive Photos

Edited by Lori Kinstad Pupeza
Contributing editors: Alan and Elizabeth Gergen

Library of Congress Cataloging-in-Publication Data

Joseph, Paul, 1970-
     Jimmy Carter / Paul Joseph.
     p. cm. -- (United States presidents)
     Summary: A simple biography of the thirty-ninth president of the United States,
who was recognized for his work toward a Middle East peace treaty.
     Includes index.
     ISBN 1-56239-747-8
     1. Carter, Jimmy, 1924- --Juvenile literature. 2. Presidents--United States--
Biography--Juvenile literature. [1. Carter, Jimmy, 1924- . 2. Presidents.] I.
Title. II. Series: United States presidents (Edina, Minn.)
     E873.J67 1998
     973.926'092--DC21
     [B]
                                             97-32924
                                            CIP
                                            AC

Contents

President Jimmy Carter

*I*n November 1976, Jimmy Carter was elected the 39th president of the United States. Jimmy's main goal was to return honor and pride to the president's office. Americans were unhappy with **government** after a political crime in the early 1970s known as "Watergate."

Jimmy did bring back honor and pride to the White House. He also believed in **morality,** and having the government help the poor. The voters trusted and felt comfortable with Jimmy. He was a simple man from a small farm town in the Deep South.

Jimmy became president when the U.S. **economy** was in trouble. Prices of food, gas, and many other things that people needed to live were rising. Buying a house was hard, and saving for the future was even harder.

President Jimmy Carter

When his first **term** as president ended, Jimmy ran for **re-election**. But he lost his job to Ronald Reagan. Many people blamed Jimmy for the **economic** problems.

Even though he lost the election, Jimmy continued to do what he did best—give back to his country. Even today, the honest and simple man always known as Jimmy continues to help the poor—and remains an image of honor and pride in America.

Opposite page: Jimmy Carter has been a long-time supporter of charities such as Habitat for Humanity.

Jimmy Carter (1924-)
Thirty-ninth President

BORN:	October 1, 1924
PLACE OF BIRTH:	Plains, Georgia
ANCESTRY:	English, Irish
FATHER:	James Earl Carter, Sr. (1894-1953)
MOTHER:	Lillian Gordy Carter (1898-1983)
WIFE:	Rosalynn Smith (1927-)
CHILDREN:	Four: 3 boys, 1 girl
EDUCATION:	Plains High School, Plains, Georgia; Georgia Southwestern College; Georgia Institute of Technology; B.S. (1946) United States Naval Academy; Union College, Schenectady, New York
RELIGION:	Baptist
OCCUPATION:	Farmer, warehouseman, businessman
MILITARY SERVICE:	Lieutenant Commander, U.S. Navy (1946-1953)
POLITICAL PARTY:	Democrat

OFFICES HELD: Chairman, Sumter County Board of
Education; Member Georgia State Senate;
Governor of Georgia

AGE AT INAUGURATION: 52

TERMS SERVED: One (1977-1981)

VICE PRESIDENT: Walter Mondale

Detail Area

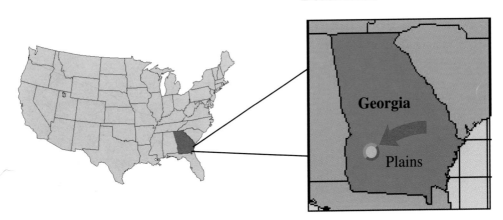

Birthplace of Jimmy Carter

Little Jimmy

*J*ames Earl Carter Jr. was born on October 1, 1924, in Plains, a small farm town in Georgia. Jimmy was the first president born in a hospital. Before that time, most people were born at home.

Jimmy was the oldest son of James Earl Sr. and Lillian Carter. Jimmy had two sisters, Gloria and Ruth. He also had a brother, William, known as Billy.

Jimmy's father served in the United States Army during World War I. After the war, James Earl Sr. ran his family farm and operated a small general store in Archery, Georgia. In the 1930s, peanuts replaced cotton as the main crop in Georgia. James Earl Sr. began to grow peanuts.

Jimmy's mother was a nurse. She was very smart and read a lot of books. She also was very caring and giving. Many times, she would go to people's houses in the middle of the night and help them when they were sick.

Jimmy and his family lived in a small house without plumbing and electricity. The Carters were one of only two families in town who weren't African American. Jimmy's friends and playmates were mostly black children.

Education, hard work, and religion were important to the Carter family. The Carters were members of the Plains Baptist Church.

Jimmy Carter at six months old with his mother Lillian

Education and Rosalynn

*J*immy attended public schools. He was the first member of the Carter family to graduate from high school—and at the top of his class.

While in high school, Jimmy decided he wanted to go to the United States Naval Academy in Annapolis, Maryland. In 1943, he was accepted into the Naval Academy.

Jimmy was an excellent student at the Naval Academy. He liked military studies and training. He finished near the top of his class.

During his final year at the Academy, Jimmy began dating his sister's best friend. Eleanor Rosalynn Smith, known as Rosalynn, was a lot like Jimmy. She came from a family who settled in a small Georgia town.

Jimmy married Rosalynn the summer after he graduated from the Naval Academy. Jimmy spent more than six years as a naval officer. In 1948, he was accepted for submarine duty.

Jimmy moved up the ranks very quickly in the navy. He and his wife moved throughout the United States for his naval career. Later, he became a lieutenant. It looked like Jimmy had an excellent naval career ahead of him. Then tragedy struck, and Jimmy had to give up his career. He and Rosalynn were going back home to Georgia.

Jimmy and Rosalynn Carter leaving their wedding reception, 1946

A Business and Family Man

*I*n 1953, Jimmy's father died. At that time, his father was a member of the Georgia House of Representatives. People throughout the state were very sad about the death of Earl Carter Sr.

Jimmy saw how his father had touched people's lives through his service to his community and state. Jimmy decided that he wanted to model his life after his father's. He quit the navy and returned to Plains to run the family business and get involved in local government.

By this time, Jimmy and Rosalynn had three sons. Because Jimmy had to move so much with the navy, each son was born in a different state.

The Carter family was happy to have one place to call home. When Jimmy returned to Georgia, he worked hard to make the family business successful.

Jimmy became involved in local government. He tried to **integrate** schools and churches in the area, but failed. Jimmy also served on the school board. Then he entered the race for the state senate. In 1962, he was elected state senator.

As a state senator, Jimmy watched over the budget and did not waste taxpayers' money. He also believed in programs that helped the poor. People loved his ideas and **re-elected** him in 1964. Jimmy, however, believed he could help more people and do more for the state if he ran for a higher office.

Jimmy Carter working in the warehouse at his peanut farm

The Making of the 39th United States President

1924
Born October 1 in Plains, Georgia

1943
Accepted into the Naval Academy

1946
Marries Rosalynn Smith on July 7

1948
Accepted for submarine duty

1962
Elected state senator of Georgia

1964
Re-elected state senator

1966
Loses Democratic primary for governor

1967
Has fourth child, a girl named Amy

1976
Elected 39th president of the United States

1977
Department of Energy is established

1978
Summit meeting—Carter initiates Middle East peace treaty

1980
Carter loses presidential election to Ronald Reagan

PRESIDENTIAL YEARS

Jimmy Carter

"I have no new dream to set forth today, but rather urge a fresh faith in the old dream."

1950
Assigned senior officer for the USS K-1

1952
Becomes lieutenant in the navy

1953
Carter's father dies; Carter quits the navy

Historical Highlights
during Carter Administration

★ Department of Energy established

★ Iran takes more than 50 hostages at the U.S. Embassy in Tehran, Iran

★ "Freedom Flotilla" brings Cuban refugees to the U.S.

★ United States boycotts Summer Olympics in Moscow

1970
Elected governor of Georgia

1974
Returns to work in the peanut business

1981
Becomes a professor at Emory University in Atlanta

1989
Watches over elections in Central America

1990
Volunteers for Habitat for Humanity— building homes for the poor

Governor Carter

*I*n 1966, Jimmy announced that he would run for governor. He lost the **Democratic** primary, however, and didn't get a chance to run. Jimmy wasn't discouraged. Right away, he made plans to run again in 1970.

In 1967, the Carters had their fourth child, a girl named Amy. Jimmy continued to run his business, help the community, and spend time with his family. He also **campaigned** for the governor's office.

Jimmy was elected the governor of Georgia in November 1970. He took office when he was **inaugurated** in January 1971. Jimmy was much different than most southern governors. He supported **integration** and chose many African Americans for state government jobs.

As governor, Jimmy traveled a lot. Many people told him he could become the president of the United States. In

1971, Jimmy began **campaigning** for president. He hired a staff and advisers.

When his **term** ended in 1974, Jimmy returned to work at his peanut business. Less than a year later, he would begin his national campaign for president of the United States.

Jimmy and Rosalynn with daughter Amy

The 39th President

*J*immy was not known as well as the other **Democratic candidates** who were running for president in 1976. But Jimmy appealed to many different kinds of people.

Jimmy was **conservative** when it came to spending money. But he was **liberal** when dealing with social problems. Because of his wide range of views, many kinds of people liked Jimmy.

At a national meeting in New York City, Democrats chose Jimmy Carter as their candidate for president. Jimmy chose U.S. Senator Walter F. Mondale from Minnesota as his vice presidential running mate.

Jimmy **campaigned** as an honest man whom people could trust. Many voters felt that the **government** needed a change because of a political crime that happened during the 1972 election.

Jimmy Carter with running mate Walter Mondale

Burglars had been caught breaking into the **Democratic** party's main office in the Watergate building in Washington, D.C. Some **Republicans** had hired the burglars to steal political secrets that might help President Richard Nixon's **re-election**. The crime became known as "Watergate."

The 1976 election for president was the closest election in more than 60 years. Jimmy won a very narrow victory. The small-town boy from Plains, who tried to follow in his father's footsteps, took one giant step. He became the 39th president of the United States.

Jimmy Carter's inauguration in January 1977

Running the Country

*J*immy became president during one of the worst winters in U.S. history. Because the weather was so cold, people used a lot of natural gas for heat. This caused a shortage, which became known as the energy crisis.

Even worse, the U.S. **economy** was in trouble. Prices for food, clothes, houses, and other things that people need to live were high, and Americans lost their jobs.

Jimmy had more success helping other countries. He held meetings in Europe and Japan to help their economies. Jimmy and the First Lady Rosalynn also traveled to South America, Africa, Asia, and the Middle East to work on world peace.

In 1978, Jimmy made history by holding a meeting between Israeli Prime Minister Menachem Begin and Egyptian President Anwar el-Sadat. In the end, Jimmy put together a Middle East peace treaty.

In 1979, near the end of Jimmy's four-year **term** as president, over fifty Americans working in the U.S. Embassy in Iran were taken **hostage**. They would not be released for more than a year.

Problems with Iran and the U.S. **economy** hurt Jimmy's **re-election campaign.** In November 1980, Jimmy lost the election for president to Ronald Reagan.

Jimmy Carter with Menachem Begin (right) and Anwar el-Sadat

A True Leader

Since he was voted out of office, Jimmy has been a professor at Emory University in Atlanta. He also has done volunteer work, and has written many books. Most of the money he has made from writing has been given to charities.

Jimmy still travels to many countries to help world peace, give advice, and to help solve world problems.

Jimmy and Rosalynn's biggest effort today is Habitat For Humanity. Jimmy and other volunteers build homes for poor people throughout the country.

Jimmy Carter worked hard for many years and accomplished more than most people. He had an excellent career in the navy, and turned a small peanut farm into a very large and successful business. In politics, he moved up the ladder faster than he did in the navy. In less than 20 years in **elected** office, Jimmy became president of the United States.

Jimmy Carter always did things the right way. He never took shortcuts and always did things with honesty. As a navy officer, as a politician, as a businessman, as the president, as a volunteer, and as a family man, Jimmy Carter truly led by example.

Jimmy visits Eastern Zaire to help Rwandan refugees.

A Man Named
Jimmy Carter

•Presidents Jimmy Carter, Richard Nixon, Gerald Ford, Ronald Reagan, and George Bush were together for the opening of the Reagan Library.   For the first time in history, five U.S. presidents met in one place.

•Jimmy Carter's brother, Billy, who was a partner in the family peanut business, was allergic to peanuts.

•At the age of 12, Carter knew that he wanted to be in the navy. He was afraid that his flat feet might keep him out of the navy, so he would stand on Coke bottles and roll back and forth to strengthen his arches.

•While in the navy, Jimmy Carter suffered from seasickness. When he had to stand watch, he carried a bucket.

•For one single party during Jimmy Carter's **term**, the White House pastry chef baked 18,000 cookies.

Jimmy Carter in the middle surrounded by four other presidents. From left to right: Bush, Reagan, Ford, and Nixon.

Glossary

Campaign—to give speeches and tell people your ideas so they will vote you into an elected office.

Candidate—a person who is running for a political office such as a the president's office.

Conservative—a person who is not open to change. They believe that the government should stay out of people's lives and that people should help themselves.

Democratic—one of the two main political parties in the United States. Democrats are known to be more liberal and believe in more government.

Economic—dealing with how much or how little money people or governments have.

Election—a process where people can vote for an elected official.

Government—many different groups who run the country, state, city, or county. The president of the United States is the highest government official.

Hostage—a person taken by force to secure the taker's demands.

Inflation—when there is an increase in money and credit that makes the prices of everyday products rise.

Inaugurate—to be sworn into a political office.

Integrate—putting African Americans and white Americans together in certain situations such as schools, churches, etc.

Liberal—a person who is very open to change. They believe that the government should help the people.

Morality—being honest and doing things the right way.

Nuclear—power that is charged through atomic energy.

Republican—one of two main political parties in the United States. Republicans are known to be more conservative and believe in less government.

Term—a length of time that a thing lasts.

Internet Sites

United States Presidents Information Page
http://we.got.net/docent/soquel/prez.htm
Links to information about United States presidents. This site is very informative, with biographies on every president as well as speeches and debates, and other links.

The Presidents of the United States of America
http://www.whitehouse.gov/WH/glimpse/presidents/html/presidents.html
This site is from the White House. With an introduction from President Bill Clinton and biographies that include each president's inaugural address, this site is excellent. Get information on White House history, art in the White House, first ladies, first families, and much more.

POTUS—Presidents of the United States
http://www.ipl.org/ref/POTUS/
In this resource you will find background information, election results, cabinet members, presidency highlights, and some odd facts on each of the presidents. Links to biographies, historical documents, audio and video files, and other presidential sites are also included to enrich this site.

These sites are subject to change. Go to your favorite search engine and type in United States presidents for more sites.

Pass It On

History Enthusiasts: educate readers around the country by passing on information you've learned about presidents or other important people who've changed history. Share your little-known facts and interesting stories. We want to hear from you!

To get posted on the ABDO Publishing Company Web site E-mail us at "History@abdopub.com"
Visit the ABDO Publishing Company Web site at www.abdopub.com

Index